Wanking

The Definitive Guide
Man's UK

D1638780

Crombie Jardine
PUBLISHING LIMITED

13 Nonsuch Walk, Cheam, Surrey, SM2 7LG
www.crombiejardine.com

First published by
Crombie Jardine Publishing Limited in 2004
Reprinted, 2005

ISBN 1-905102-00-3

Original concept and compilation by Crombie Jardine
Designed by 'Mr Stiffy'
Printed and bound in the United Kingdom by
William Clowes Ltd, Beccles, Suffolk.

CONTENTS

Wank

Usually considered a taboo word
= masturbate

Masturbate

More acceptable than 'wank'
= arouse oneself

INTRODUCTION

About five years ago I set up Wankers Anonymous and there are now over 300 branches throughout the English-speaking world.

Many men have been brought up to believe that wanking is evil and wrong. Wankers Anonymous – by allowing men to talk openly in a group session – has helped them on many levels. To be able to stand up and say, "Hello, my name is Roger* and I am a wanker!" can be a truly liberating experience. For some, time spent wanking has been filled with guilt and fear. Too many men think that they are the only wankers in the world. This little book will go some way to prove that *all* men are wankers.

I hope you enjoy it and if you would like to share your wanking experiences with me, please email me at palmaction@crombiejardine.com.

Dick Palmer
September 2004

* This is not his real name (which is actually Martin).

EXTRACT FROM THE MINUTES OF THE INAUGURAL MEETING OF WANKERS ANONYMOUS, PRATT'S BOTTOM, KENT, ENGLAND, JANUARY 2004.

Thirty-two people were present on a stormy, windy night. The meeting was chaired by Dick Palmer. After reading out the draft constitution of Wankers Anonymous, Dick opened the meeting and asked for the first member's contribution.

Hello, my name is Paul and I am a wanker. Even though I've been married 12 years, I still secretly masturbate daily. It has got so bad that I have started using strange, exotic fruit in my quest for the ultimate wank. Can you help me?

Dick responded by saying that no guilt whatsoever should be associated with wanking; after all, that is what we have a right hand for (or a left hand if you are left-handed). However, great care must be taken when using strange, exotic fruit.

A close friend of Dick's once got a pip from a watermelon stuck in his penis, causing great discomfort. A visit to his doctor caused him great embarrassment and the doctor much mirth.

Hello, my name is James and I am a wanker. When I was 14, I was furiously wanking over an edition of Big & Busty when, unbeknown to me, my mother entered my bedroom and saw quite clearly what I was up to. I am in a relationship now where my girlfriend wants me to masturbate in front of her whilst she masturbates in front of me. I am unable to do this as the image of my mother looking down at me many years ago causes me such mental anguish. Please help me.

A member called Frank, who had a similar experience, suggested the only way round this was hypnosis; where the mental picture of James's mother would be changed to that of his present partner. Dick suggested that if that didn't work, James should try wearing a blindfold.

Hello, my name is Gary and I am a really big wanker. Wanking for me has become the most time-consuming part of my life. Some days I masturbate 14 or 15 times and this is having a massive negative effect on my job as a London bus driver. What can I do?!

Four or five members said they wished they could masturbate that many times a day and some silly remarks were made. Dick brought the meeting to order by saying that an elastic band tied tightly around the scrotum area whilst Gary was at work might prove successful.

If you have a wanking story or dilemma that you'd like to share, please email Dick at palmaction2004@yahoo.co.uk.

EUPHEMISMS

Adjusting your set
Auditioning the finger puppets

Backstroke roulette
Bashing the Bishop
Bashing the candle
Beating off
Beating the dummy
Beating your meat
Being your own best friend

Blowing the load
Boxing the bald champ
Buffing the banana
Burping the baby

Charming the snake
Choking Kojak
Choking the bald guy until he pukes
Choking the chicken
Creaming your cock
Crowning the king
Cruising for an oozing

Doin' the solitary rhumba
Doing a hand job
Doing handiwork
Doing it your way
Doing the five-knuckle shuffle

Electing the President

Firing the canon

Fist fucking
Fisting your mister
Five on one
Flogging the bishop
Flogging the dog
Flogging the salami
Flute solo
Freeing Willy
Frigging

Getting off
Getting the German soldier marching

Getting your palm red
Getting your pole varnished
Getting your rocks off
Grappling the gorilla
Greasing the pipe

H

Hans Solo
Hand job
Handy work
Hand to gland combat
Hard labour
Having a date with Fisty Palmer

Having a one-night-stand with yourself
Having it off
Having sex with someone you love
Having the urge for a surge
Holding the sausage hostage
Humping the hose

Ironing some wrinkles

Jacking off

Jerkin' the gherkin
Jerking the joy stick
Jerking off
Juicing the joy stick
Just jerkin' it

Kicking seamen

Launching the hand shuttle
Letting the juice loose

Loving the muppet
Lubing the tube

M

Making out with yourself
Making the bald man puke
Mangling the midget
Manual labour
Manual override
Meeting Rosie Hancock
Milking one's self
Milking the bull
Milking the cow

One gun salute
One off the wrist

Packing your palm
Peeling the banana
Playing a little five-on-one
Playing in a one-man show
Playing pocket pool
Playing Uno
Pleasing the Pope

Pocket pinball
Pocket pool
Polishing the helmet
Polishing the sword
Polishing your knob
Popping the cork
Pounding off
Pulling off
Pulling the pole
Pulling your prick
Pumping the muscle
Pumping the piston
Pumping the python

Ramming the ham
Rolling your own
Romeo and Himself
Rubbing off
Rubbing one out

Sacrificing sperm to the god of lonely
nights
Secret handshake
Self-induced penile regurgitation
Self-inflicted intercourse

Sex with someone you really love
Shagging
Shaking hands with Yul Brenner
Shaking the bottle
Shaking the sauce
Shaking the sausage
Shining your pole
Shooting off
Slamming the ham
Slamming the spam
Slapping it
Slapping the clown
Slapping the donkey
Slapping the salami

Smacking off
Snapping the monkey
Solo flight
Solo marathon
Solo sex
Spanking the bishop
Spanking the monkey
Spanking the salami
Spanking the wank
Squeezing the juice
Squeezing the weasel
Straining the main vein
Strangling the Serpent
Stroking it

Stroking off
Stroking the dog
Stroking the lizard
Stroking the satin-headed serpent
Stroking your meat
Stroking your poker

Taking a shake break
Taking matters into your own hands
Taunting the one-eyed weasel
Tenderizing the meat
Testing the testicles

That crazy hand jive
Thumping the pump
Tickling your fancy
Tickling the pickle
Tossing off
Tossing the turkey
Twanging the wire
Twisting your crank

Unloading the gun

Varnishing the flagpole

Wacking off
Wacking the one-eyed worm
Wacking the weasel
Wacking the willie
Waking the dead
Waking Wee Willie Wonka
Walking the Snake
Wanking

Wanking with the one-eyed
wonder weasel
Washing the meat
Whackin' the weasel
Whacking it
Whacking off
Whacking Willy
Whipping the one-eyed trouser snake
Whipping the rat
Whipping the stiff
Whipping your dripper
Working off
Wrestling the eel
Wrestling the purple-headed warrior

Yanking off
Yanking the crank
Yanking your plank

Posh People's Euphemisms

Boxing with Richard

Capturing the Bishop

Digitally oscillating one's penis

Engaging in safe sex

Getting a hand job

Getting to know oneself

Going blind

Masturbating

My sex life!

Onanism (a biblical term)

Playing with your penis

Playing with yourself

Relieving tension

Safe sex

Taking part in population control

Talking quietly to yourself

'Star Wars' Euphemisms for Wanking

**Test Firing the
Death Star**

**Scratching Yoda
Behind the Ears**

**Polishing
Vader's Helmet**

Performing the
Jedi Hand Trick

Unsheathing the Meatsaber

*Manually Targeting
the Rebel Base*

*Releasing the
Special Edition*

*Communicating with
Red Leader One*

*Tinkering with
the R2 Unit*

ONE-LINERS

Practice safe sex, go f*** yourself.

Procrastination is like wanking: at first it might feel great, but in the end you're just f***ing yourself.

97% of people wank; the other 3% don't have hands.

Sex is like bridge: all you need is a good partner or a good hand.

Wanking: a completely self-taught skill.

Masturbate in the shower too much and you'll get an erection every time it rains!

MASTURBATION
Q & A

What is it?

Sexual self-stimulation, often by hand. Commonly known as "wanking" in the UK and "jacking off" in the USA.

And 'mutual' masturbation?
The manual stimulation of one person by another. Otherwise known as "manual sex".

What is a circle jerk?
Group masturbation – wanking in a group of two or more people.

"Jack-and-Jills"?
"Jacks" – group wanking clubs or parties for men only; "Jills" – parties or clubs for women only; "Jack-and-Jills" – for both sexes.

What's the best way for a guy to do it?
Usually by wrapping the fingers around the erect penis and then stroking it up and down until ejaculation. Alternatively, by rubbing the erect penis against something until ejaculation.

Can I do it too much?
Generally, no. (Good eh?!)

Will my penis get larger/smaller when I have a wank?
Well, larger, yes. But smaller once you've finished!

Will I catch anything from masturbation?

Er . . . no. You cannot give yourself a sexually transmitted disease by playing with yourself.

Will I go blind / bald / insane / get hairy palms / develop chronic fatigue / cause my penis to shrivel and fall off from wanking?

No. Come on. These are scare tactics to discourage you from doing it.

Can a doctor tell if I've been wanking?

No.

Can my partner tell if I've been wanking?

It depends whether you've still got that satisfied grin on your face or not.

Will masturbating affect my sexual performance?

Not likely. Why should it make any difference?

Will I become obsessed with masturbation?

It's always possible. Stop worrying about becoming obsessed with it or you'll be obsessing about being obsessed and get yourself in a right state. If you really think you might have a problem, go and see your GP.

Isn't masturbation just for losers who can't get a shag?

Oh, grow up.

Will I burn in hell for masturbating?

If you seriously have to ask this question, you might want to talk to your minister.

Is my penis big enough?

If you can wank, it is big enough.

What is "blue balls"?

"Blue balls" (although they don't actually turn blue . . . More like purple. –ish) is painful; your balls feel on fire because of prolonged sexual arousal. The whole area gets flushed with blood and changes colour. If the pain hasn't started, stop whatever it is you're doing for a bit. If it's too late on the pain front, forget actually doing it – it will most likely hurt. A lot. Really.

MASTURBATION & RELIGION

BLOWING THE LID ON THE GREAT TABOO

What exactly is the Church's problem with wanking? How cum it is shocking and sinful still, when compared to many other things going on in today's permissive society, it is HARMLESS!

Look at all the benefits – both physical and emotional for men and women:

- It is a normal, natural activity

- It relieves tension, emotional stress and anxiety

- It stops you from exploding in inappropriate ways

- It's a safe, legitimate way to satisfy your sexual needs without indulging in harmful or illegal activities

- For men, it's good for the prostate and can prevent painful prostate congestion

- It's Nature's way of saying "use it or lose it": a good wank gets rid of old sperm and keeps the ejaculates balanced, guaranteeing fresh, strong sperm for mating. Fantastic!

- Self-awareness gained from masturbation makes it a central feature of many sex therapy programmes

- It has been shown to have a healthy effect on the immune system

- It's free

- It's easy to do (no special skills needed)

- It can be done anywhere that is private (or semi-private if that gets you going)

- You can be totally selfish here and not worry about the "was it good for you, darling?"

- It doesn't need to take loads of time

- It isn't fattening (girls)

- It's not illegal (is it?)

- It's not immoral (those who say it is also do it but just lie about it, because that makes them feel better)

- You get a high without drugs

- It doesn't produce any children

- It feels great!

- And NO you won't go mad, blind, bald, get hairy palms, or anything like that. You are a normal, competent member of society – despite all the time you've spent devoted to it!

SO – what IS all the fuss about?
It all seems to have started with the
misunderstanding of the biblical passage
related to Onan. Onan's sin, actually,
had nothing to do with masturbation
being wrong. His problem was that
he didn't get his dead brother's wife
pregnant (it's a long story). Then came
the unacceptable Christian interpretation
that sex was only proper for procreation,
not enjoyment alone. And there you have
it . . . masturbation gets its bad name.

One of the basic rules the Bible gives is

don't have sex with someone you aren't married to. Apparently Jesus taught that looking at a woman with lust was as bad as committing adultery with her, i.e. the thought was as bad as the deed. So, when you masturbate, if you imagine you are having sex with someone who you aren't married to, then you're breaking one of God's laws. Yes, really.

And so developed the Church's teaching that thinking about sex (which you're obviously going to do when you're wanking) is evil whether you action this thought or not (most people would say then you might as well go for it!).

There's no sin in fantasizing.

Wanking is not a sin. It is only cultural brainwashing by the Church in an attempt to control people's behaviour that has taught us otherwise.

RELIGIOUS EUPHEMISMS FOR THE GREAT 'M' WORD

Banging the Bishop

Baptizing John

Blessed Relief

Bopping Bishop

Diddling the Diocese

Fondling the fundamentalist

Fondling the Pharaoh

Greasing the Grail

Humping the Halo

Jarring Jehovah

Jostling the apostle

Juicing the Judas

Lighting the altar candle

Milking Mohammed

Mounting the Mormon

Pounding Paul's Peter

Preparing the holy water

Priming the Pagan

Rubbing the Rabbi

Sailing the Arc

Seizing Caesar

Spunking the monk

Stroking the steeple

Taming Goliath

Testicular Testament

Working for the second coming

Zapping the Zoroastrian

RIDDLES

Q: What's the difference between an egg and a good wank?

A: You can beat an egg.

Q: What is a Yankee?

A: The same thing as a quickie, but a man can do it by himself!

Q: What made Pinocchio realize he was made of wood?

A: Splinters.

Q: **What is the worst kind of rejection?**

A: When your hand falls asleep as you're masturbating.

Q: **If lovers celebrate Valentine's Day, what do wankers celebrate?**

A: Palm Sunday.

Q: **Which of the senses is most alert during wanking?**

A: Your hearing — listening out for footsteps.

Q: What's the difference between pink and purple?

A: Your grip!

Q: What's the difference between hard and light?

A: You can get to sleep with a light on.

Q: What do wanking and a three-putt have in common?

A: You're ashamed, but you know you'll do it again!

JOKES

Three sales reps get snowed in on a farm and have to spend the night in the farmer's house. As there aren't enough bedrooms to go round, one of the reps has to sleep in the attic. The farmer is a trusting soul and allows his two daughters to share their rooms with the reps.

Before turning in, the reps discuss whether or not they are going to get lucky. They devise a code so that they can let each other know how they've got on. Rep 1 says he'll make the sound of a train and shout, "Freight train through bedroom one!" and Rep 2 says he'll call out, "Mail train through bedroom two!"

Sometime after going to bed, the shout, "Freight train through bedroom one!" is heard. A little while after that comes the cry, "Mail train through bedroom two!" Not wanting to be outdone, Rep 3 in the attic blurts out, "Handcar through the attic!"

Penis and Toe are talking one day. Toe is complaining, "Man, I have a hard life. Every day I'm stuck inside a smelly shoe, and because my master is clumsy, I always get hurt and sore." Penis sighs and responds, "You call that a hard life?! My master makes me do push-ups until I throw up!"

A married couple goes to see a new film at the cinema. The woman is uncomfortable watching some of the sex scenes, particularly a masturbation one. As they are coming out of the cinema, she voices her opinion, "I didn't really enjoy that, you know – I'm sorry, but I find masturbation in a film really offensive." Her husband sighs, looks slightly shame-faced and says, "All right, I'm sorry — I won't do it again."

A man goes to get his eyesight tested. The optician says, "You should stop masturbating." The man asks, "Why? It doesn't really make you go blind, does it?" The optician replies, "No, but it's disturbing people in the waiting room."

A nurse is doing her rounds on the psychiatric ward and sees one of her patients, Jim, pretending to drive a car. "Hey, Jim, what's happening?" she asks. "Just driving to the coast!" he replies, eeping an imaginary horn. She smiles, waves and wishes him a safe journey and leaves the room.

Later on she checks on Jim again and he is just getting out of his non-existent car. "Great run," he says, "I just love it when you get down to the sea!" The nurse smiles and leaves him to it. She goes down the corridor, only to find Mark lying on his bed, wanking like mad. "Um, Mark – what are you doing?" she asks. Mark looks up and grins, "Screwing Jim's wife whilst he's down at the coast!"

A father comes home after a long hard day, drops his briefcase on the floor and heads to the fridge for a beer. As he's walking back into the lounge he hears a faint moaning coming from his daughter's bedroom. Curious, he tiptoes down the corridor and pauses outside her bedroom door. Sure enough – moaning.

He pushes the door open slowly and sees

his daughter on the bed, eyes closed, using a vibrator and just about to climax. Shocked, he shouts, "What the hell are you doing?!"

She quickly grabs the sheet and wraps it round her, yelling at him to get out and let her put some clothes on.

He goes back to the lounge, stunned, and turns on the TV, waiting for her to come in. When she does, she says, "Listen, Dad. You should've knocked. I'm 29 years old, I haven't had a boyfriend and probably never will at this rate. I have needs, all right?"

Her father says, "I'm sorry. I'm sure you'll get a boyfriend soon." She replies, "No, Dad. It's just not going to happen. I know it. I'll never ever get married. So, I'm sorry to disappoint you."

A week or so later, the daughter comes home early one afternoon to find her father sitting on the living room sofa, watching TV, with a gin and tonic in one hand, and the vibrator in the other. "Dad!" she yells, "What the hell do you think YOU'RE doing?"

He looks casually over his shoulder at her and says, "What does it look like I'm doing? I'm having a drink with my son-in-law."

A man and a woman are sitting next to each other on a plane that's taxiing down the runway. Suddenly he sneezes violently, undoes his zip and wipes the end of his penis with a tissue. He does up his zip and opens the in-flight magazine and begins to read. The woman is shocked.

A few minutes later the same thing happens. This time she has to say something. "Excuse me, but your behaviour is disgusting — if you do that once more I am going to call the stewardess and have you removed from this plane."

He replies, "I'm so sorry, but I have this very rare and extremely embarrassing physical handicap that makes me have an orgasm every time I sneeze."

The woman, taken aback by the man's honesty and now embarrassed by her outburst, says, "Oh God, no, I'm sorry, you poor man. Are you taking anything for it?"

"Yes," he answers, "Pepper."

Charlie comes home from school and his mother asks him what he has learned that day. "Oh, wow, we learned about sex today!" he replies, enthusiastically. His mother is slightly taken aback and later on tells her husband about the conversation.

They discuss it and agree that sex education at school is a good thing and that she shouldn't worry about anything.

Later that evening, she asks her husband to call Charlie for dinner. He walks past Charlie's room and sees him wanking furiously on the bed. "After you finish your homework, come down for dinner, son."

✳

One day a university lecturer was giving his undergraduates a revision session. He had prepared all the notes, photocopied important fact sheets and handed them out in class. "Right, listen up!" he said, "I shan't accept any excuses for work not handed in. I don't care if the dog ate it, you had to work, you partied all night, etc. No excuse is going to be accepted."

"What about sexual exhaustion?" piped up one cocky student.

"No way!" said the lecturer, "You'll just have to learn how to write with your other hand!"

Adam was going through a stage where he couldn't please his wife in bed. He went to see his GP who suggested he masturbated before having sex. Adam really wanted to make things work with his wife, and he liked the GP's suggestion, so on his way home he thought, "I'll just stop off here, round the corner, and have a quick session before I get home." He pulled into a layby, got under the car, lay on the ground, closed his eyes and procceded to "check the axle".

After about 10 minutes he felt a tug on his trouser leg and asked, "Yes, who is it?" "Police. Do you mind telling me what you're doing, sir?" With his eyes still closed, Adam replied, "Hi officer. Yes . . . I'm checking my car's axle." "Right," came the reply, "Well, I suggest you check your brakes while you're at it, because your car rolled down the hill about 5 minutes ago."

In 1993, the American Government funded a study to see why the head of a man's penis was larger than the shaft. One year and $180,000 later, it concluded that the reason was to give the man more pleasure during sex.

In 1994, France decided to do her own study. Three years and FF 400,000 later, it was concluded that the reason was to give the woman more pleasure during sex.

Poland, unsatisfied with both these

findings, conducted her own study.
Two weeks and US $75.46 later, it was
concluded that it was to keep man's
hand from flying off and hitting him
in the forehead.

One day the president of a large bank
called his vice-president, Mr. Smith, into
his office and said, "We've no choice but
to make some cutbacks. Either Jack or Jill
will have to be laid off."

Mr Smith looked at the president pensively and replied, "Jill is a loyal, hardworking employee, but Jack has a wife and kids. It's a very difficult choice to make."

The next morning Mr. Smith waited for his employees to arrive. Jill was in the office before anyone else, so Mr. Smith took the opportunity and said, "Jill, listen . . . I've got a problem. You see, I've got to lay you or Jack off and I don't know what to do."

Quick as a flash Jill replied, "You'd better

jack off. I've got a headache."

Two women friends always rode their bicycles together. One day, when going a different route to normal, one of the women remarked, "I've never come this way before." To which her friend replied, "Must be the cobblestones!"

A 40-year-old man walks into a large West End chemist, approaches the girl behind the nearest counter and asks "Can I buy condoms here, please?" "Yes," she says, "What size are you?" "Well, I don't rightly know," he replies.

So she leans over the counter, unzips his trousers, has a feel, and then says over the intercom, "EXTRA LARGE CONDOMS TO TILL 3 PLEASE. EXTRA LARGE CONDOMS TO TILL 3." The man grins. The condoms are brought over, the man pays and leaves.

A 25-year-old man then comes into the chemist and walks up to the same counter. He asks the girl, "Do you sell condoms here?" She replies, "Yes we do. What size do you need?" He says, "Um . . . I don't know."

So she leans over, unzips his trousers, takes a couple of tugs, and then says over the intercom, "LARGE CONDOMS TO TILL 3 PLEASE. LARGE CONDOMS TO TILL 3." The man smiles. Again, the condoms are brought over, the man pays for them and leaves.

Seeing this, a 15-year-old boy, hoping to get lucky, goes up to the girl at till number 3 and asks sheepishly, "Um, ah... do you sell condoms here?" "Yep," she says, "What size do you need?" "I don't know," he shrugs.

So she unzips his trousers for a feel, pauses, and says over the intercom, "CLEAN UP AT TILL 3 PLEASE. CLEAN UP AT TILL 3!"

Pinocchio and new girlfriend had just had sex for the first time. New to all this, Pinocchio asked her tentatively, "So . . . how was I?" She didn't want to upset him, and so tried to put it gently, "Well, Pinocchio . . . I hate to say this, but you've given me splinters!"

Pinocchio was devastated. He went crying to Gepetto. "My girlfriend says that I gave her splinters when we had sex! Is there anything you can do?"

Gepetto says, "What you need, my boy, is a piece of sandpaper. Use this once a day, and it'll solve your problem."

A few weeks later, Gepetto bumped into Pinocchio in the street. "Did the sandpaper do the trick? Is everything ok with your girlfriend now?" he asked.

"Girlfriend?" Pinocchio asked, "Who needs girlfriends?"

A couple of friends went to a special preview of a modern art exhibition and saw a painting of three dark-skinned men, all naked, sitting on a park bench. All three men looked very similar, but the man sitting in the middle had a pink penis. The friends were discussing the painting, trying to work it out, just as the artist walked past. "Can I help you with this painting?" he asked. "Well . . . yes, actually," said the first friend, "How come the man in the middle has a pink penis?"

"Oh," said the artist, "They're coal miners, and the one in the middle went home for lunch."

Two friends are coming out of the gym. One is complaining about a pain in his arm and saying he'll just have to take time off work and go and see his GP. His friend says, "I wouldn't bother – there's a great machine in the chemist's round the corner. All you have to do is take a urine sample, put the bottle in the machine and it will analyze it for you – then and there." The guy thinks it's worth a shot, so goes to the chemist the next day, does as he's instructed and the machine churns out a piece of paper saying, "You have tennis elbow. Rest your arm for two weeks."

The guy thinks, "Wow! This is amazing!" Then, being the mischievous kind of person he is, he thinks about tricking the machine. After all, he says to himself, how difficult can it be?

So he goes home and mixes up some tap water, some of his dog's poo, and his wife's urine — and to top it off he masturbates into the mixture. Delighted, he goes down to the drugstore and puts in the sample.

The machine churns around for a moment, and then it spits out a piece of paper that says, "Firstly, your tap water is hard. Secondly, your dog has worms. Thirdly, your wife is a cocaine addict. And fourthly, you'll never get rid of that tennis elbow if you keep masturbating!"

Three male friends go on a skiing trip

together and, because of a double-booking mix-up at the resort, they end up having to share a double bed together, as there aren't enough in the chalet to go round.

In the middle of the night, the guy on the right wakes up and says, "I had this crazy, wild dream I was getting a hand job!"

The guy on the left wakes up and, incredibly, he's had the same dream.

Then the guy in the middle pipes up, "That's funny — I dreamed I was skiing!"

A young lady reports for her first day at work as the secretary at a sex clinic. The head doctor is showing her around, when they come across a man masturbating in the corridor. "Hey! What's going on?" the lady asks, shocked. The doctor answers, "Oh, that's Mike. He has the disease hyper-spermatogenesis. If he doesn't ejaculate half a dozen times, his testicles would swell up and explode."

She nods and they continue the tour.

Next, they pass a room where a beautiful female nurse is giving a man a blow job. "So – what's going on there?" asks the secretary. The doctor replies, "He has the same problem as Mike, except he's got private health care."

A boy is in his bedroom, just about to cum as he masturbates vigorously, when in walks his father.

"You'll go blind if you carry on with that, son," says the father.

The boy is embarrassed and promises to not do it again.

A week later, again the father walks in on the boy as he is masturbating. "Hey! I thought we agreed you were going to stop that!" he sputters angrily.

"Well," says the son, "I figured I'd stop when I needed glasses."

A cowboy is out riding when he comes across an American Indian lying on the ground – shirt open, buckskins round his ankles, complete with a perfect erection. The cowboy asks, "What are you doing?" The man replies, "I'm telling the time." The cowboy says, "I'm sorry? What do you mean?"

The Indian replies, "It's an age old custom, but a white man could never do it. See, it's like a sundial. I can tell the time by how the shadow falls."

"I see," says the cowboy. "So what time

is it?"

"Just gone 11," says the Indian.

The cowboy thanks him and rides on, marvelling at what he's just seen. Some time later, he comes across a second Indian, lying in the same position, again with a perfect erection. The cowboy asks the time.

"Almost 2:30," says the man on the ground.

"Thanks!" says the cowboy, and moves on again.

A couple of hours later, he comes across a third Indian, same position, with erection pointing skyward — only this guy is masturbating with great vigour and concentration.

The cowboy says, "Hey, I met some of your guys today, and they showed me how they tell the time — but what are YOU doing?"

"Winding the clock," he answers.

A kid is masturbating behind the garage. His dad happens to walk by and hears him. He says, "Stop that, boy! It'll make you go blind!" The boy shouts back, "Dad! I'm over here!"

One day, Ian walks in on his big brother and his girlfriend making love. He says, "What are you doing?" and his brother replies, "Playing poker — she's the queen and I'm the king." Ian leaves, not knowing any better.

About a week later, Ian walks in on his parents having sex and says, "Mum . . . Dad, what are you doing?" and his father replies, "Playing poker — she's the queen and I'm the king." Ian leaves the room, again not knowing any better.

The next day, Ian's brother walks in on him masturbating and says, "What do you think you're doing?" to which Ian replies, "Playing poker." "Where's the queen?" his brother asks. Ian looks up and grins, "Why do I need a queen when I've got a hand like this?"

David's father was a farmer and had a lot of guns around the house. He was always telling his son about the danger of guns, and how to take care of them, and so forth. One day David was in the bath masturbating, and his mother walked in just as he was ejaculating. She stormed out, and David chased after her, saying, "I wasn't playing with myself! I was just cleaning it and it went off!"

A very repressed married couple could never bring themselves to talk about sex; they always referred to it as "doing the laundry" instead.

One evening, the husband was feeling a bit horny, so he asked his wife to come upstairs and help him with the laundry. She said she had a headache and would be up later. After about an hour or so, the wife went upstairs, slipped into bed next to her husband, and said she was willing to do the laundry now. "That's all right, dear," he replied, "It was a small load, so I did it by hand."

An elderly couple wanted to have a child. Their GP told them they were a bit old to start a family, but decided to test the man for a sperm count anyway. He gave them a jar to take home and told the man to masturbate, produce a sperm sample and bring the bottle back to the office.

Two days later, the couple went back to the surgery. The man told the GP there was a problem. "I tried with my right hand, and then I tried with my left hand, but no results," he said. "Then my wife tried with her right hand and also her left hand, and she even used her mouth — with her teeth in and her teeth out — but we still couldn't get the lid off the jar."

Wanking
Achievements

A section devoted to those of you out there who don't take yourselves too seriously. Thank God for you. You know who you are.

Donald

According to Donald's calculations, he has travelled almost 680 miles along his penis. Confused? Let Don explain in his own words . . . .

"How many miles are on your pole?" you ask.

Let's say when I make a stroke it is about 2 inches up and 2 inches down, making a total of 4 inches per stroke. If I average about 500 strokes per wank, that's 2,000 inches per session. This times 365 days equals 730,000 inches per year. For an average lifetime's wanking, multiply this by 60 years: that makes 43,800,000 inches. Divide this by 12 to find out how many feet – and you've got 3,650,000 feet.

Divide this by 5,280 feet per mile and the answer is: by the time I've finished, I will have travelled 691.3 delightful miles along my sausage.

Wicked, hey?

Donald

For those of you who are health conscious: the average wank uses up 75 calories. Therefore, as part of a calorie-controlled diet, wanking is a useful way of keeping the pounds off. Tell this to your partner the next time you want to lose a few pounds.

(DP)

Bruce Smashes the World Record for Wanking!

In January 2004, Bruce Wood was crowned the new king of wanking. In an amazing feat of endurance, Bruce achieved 45 orgasms in a 24-hour period, aided and abetted by his staggeringly impressive library of over 500 films!

Taking one look at Bruce's forearm muscles it is clear that he is not your average wanker. He is quoted as saying, *"Wanking for me has become a way of* ife. It's as natural as breathing. I've een training for this since I was 11 ears old and I'm very satisfied with my erformance today of all days."

he world record for wanking was ormerly held by German student, Hans olo, who achieved 34 orgasms in one ay. Mr. Solo was not available for omment, although his agent said he was ot happy about this and he is presently n training in Bavaria to reclaim his ightful crown.

When asked what his ambition was now,

Bruce said *"My immediate aim is to get a bag of ice on my wedding tackle to soothe the burning."*

SONGS FOR CHRISTMAS

Jingle Balls

Wankers all! Wankers all!
Careful how you go
There's no shame to play the game
Just don't keep it all on show
No!

Wankers all! Wankers all!
Careful how you go
Come and have some festive fun
With Rudolph in the snow
Ho!

Oh Come all Ye Wankers

Oh come all ye Wankers
There's no harm in stroking
Oh come all ye Wankers
All over the world
Come and be happy
Rejoice at your leisure
Oh come and feel relieved
Oh come and feel relieved
Oh come and feel relieved
All through the night

My grandfather heard this wanking limerick in 1914 when he was called up for the Great War. If you've come across it and know when it was written please let me know. If you know a better limerick, I want to know about it for the next edition of this book! [DP]

MASTURBATION POEM

There was a young man called McKean
Who invented a wanking machine
On the 99th stroke
The bloody thing broke
And churned his balls to cream

FURTHER READING

**The Big Book of Masturbation:
From Angst to Zeal**
by Martha Cornog
(Down There Press, 2003)

**Exploring Your Sexual Self:
A Guided Journal**
by Joan Mazza (Noth Light Books, 2001)

**The Joy of Self-Pleasuring:
Why Feel Guilty about Feeling Good?**
by Edward L. Rowan
(Prometheus Books, 2000)

Masturbation and Adult Sexuality
by Suzanne Sarnoff and Irving Sarnoff
(Replica Books, 2001)

A Mind of Its Own: A Cultural History of the Penis
by David M. Friedman (Penguin, 2003)

More Joy: Advanced Guide to Solo Sex
by Harold Litten and Rod Jenson Shows
(illustrator) (Factor Press, 1996)

122

www.crombiejardine.com